Deer
For Kids

Amazing Animal Books
For Young Readers

By
Rachel Smith

Mendon Cottage Books

JD-Biz Publishing

Read More Amazing Animal Books

Purchase at Amazon.com

Table of Contents

Introduction

Once upon a time, the word that deer was based on meant any wild animal, and venison meant any meat caught from a wild animal. Similar words still exist in other languages besides English, but for several reasons, they didn't narrow it down to what is now a deer.

Deer are often seen as one of the most graceful kinds of animals. They live throughout the world, except in Antarctica and Australia. Women with brown eyes are often described as 'doe eyed', because most deer (does are female deer) have beautiful brown eyes.

Deer also factor into myth and legend; among many instances of deer, there comes the story of the Ancient Greek goddess Artemis, who turned a peeping hunter into a deer to punish him. Deer were also said to pull her chariot. Reindeer, another type of deer, pull Santa Claus's sleigh. Celts considered deer to be a sort of 'fairy cattle', milked and herded by fairies much like the Celts milked and herded cows.

The deer is a beautiful creature, and it's no wonder it's captured the imagination of many ancient and current thinkers.

What are deer?

A deer is a member of the family Cervidae. This covers around ninety or so different species of deer.

A doe.

A lot of terms are used to refer to deer. First, a male red deer is called a hart; not all male deer are harts, however, and it really depends on the deer species. Males can be called bulls, bucks, or stags; males that have been made unable to have babies with a female are called haviers.

Female deer can go by hind, doe, or cow. Baby deer can go by calf (usually for bigger deer) or fawn (usually for smaller deer).

Deer can be anywhere from a tiny 20 pounds to a whopping 1,000 pounds, depending on the species. The family Cervidae includes such large animals as the moose, which lives in the North, and the little muntjacs of Asia.

A group of deer is always called a herd, no matter the size or species.

Deer do not have a family unit quite like humans. The father does not raise the fawn, and in fact does absolutely nothing to help the mother. It is entirely up to the mother deer, the doe, to take care of the fawn.

What do deer look like?

Deer range in size from the tiny pudú to the gigantic moose. Most male deer have antlers; the only female deer that have antlers are caribou (also known as reindeer).

Sika deer, a doe and a fawn.

Deer are quadrupeds, meaning that they have four legs. Deer also have four-chambered stomachs, a lot like a cow. Deer have hooves, tails, and fur.

They can be different colors, though the most common color is brown. Deer can be albino, meaning that, because they have no pigment, they are white. However, a large amount of white deer are not albino, but are simply white, as a genetic mutation. This is a bit of a handicap for deer, since they don't blend in much, but they are quite popular among deer breeders and deer hunters. Another type of color of deer are piebald deer; this means they are both brown and white, in a sort of splotchy pattern.

A lot of baby deer have spots, but not all; also, some species of deer keep their spots into adulthood. There is no set way for all deer to look; with more than ninety kinds, they vary widely.

Deer have ears that move to catch sound, much like rabbits. They don't have quite the hearing of rabbits, but deer are able to pick up on sounds much more easily than humans.

Antlers are the common picture of a deer, and in several places, the deer is raised domestically for its antlers, and in some places they're raised for their meat.

These antlers are fairly interesting; a deer with antlers will have them grow under a soft sort of skin called velvet. Slowly, it calcifies (turns into a hard substance, similar to bone) under the velvet, and when it is ready, the deer rub it off.

Once it is ready, the male deer will typically use their antlers to fight other male deer. This is so that female deer, who typically live in herds, will mate with them and have their babies.

Deer don't have upper front teeth; instead, they have a tough pad. This makes it easier to chew their cud like a cow.

Most deer also have glands on their faces, right near their eyes. These are used to mark their territory; a deer leaves its scent there, and other deer are alerted to whose territory it is.

What do deer eat?

Deer are herbivores. Their mouths are designed without quite the same upper teeth humans have, because most of them are designed to eat plants.

A white tail fawn eating.

Some types of deer have long canine teeth, which makes them look a bit ferocious. One type of deer will even eat meat.

Most deer, however, need plants to eat. If they can't get leaves or grass, they will often eat the bark off of trees; that's usually during winter seasons.

A fawn will drink milk from its mother, like most mammals. Its mother will go out and graze or eat for a long time, typically, and come back to where she's hidden her fawn to feed it.

Fawns don't like being left behind, most of the time, so a mother will have to be firm with her baby and make it stay hidden. The fawn is hidden, not just because of its spots, but also because a mother deer will lick her baby clean until it has almost no scent. This keeps the baby safe while the mother grazes.

A father deer simply eats, as well as fighting other deer.

Dear do not usually eat much grass or hay; they prefer leaves the most. This is because their stomachs are more primitive compared to a cow's or a sheep's. They need easily digestible things. They also need a lot of nutritious food. So, leaves, plant shoots, new grasses, and other plants are typically in a deer's diet.

Deer prefer to browse rather than graze; this means that they are more picky about what they eat. Cows and sheep will eat whatever is in front of them; deer will pick through it.

Where do deer live?

Deer live everywhere, except Australia, Antarctica, and most of Africa. They live in the tundra, which is a kind of ground that is frozen all year, and they live in rain forests. They live in the United States and Canada, and they live in South America. In fact, the smallest and largest deer are both in the Americas.

A bull elk.

In Africa, the Barbary stag lives in a small sliver of Africa; there are some deer that have been introduced in other parts of Africa, but they are not native to Africa.

Deer depend on foliage (like trees and other plants) to eat. This means they don't usually live in the city, though with increased city areas, they often wander into the city. This is why so many of them get hit by cars.

Many deer live in areas that are sort of in between forests and prairies; this allows them greater grazing areas. Some live in mountains, and their fawns are more like goat kids (agile and more active). Others live in swamps or other places.

Each deer species is adapted to its environment, and will not frequently do well outside of it. Some are very specialized for their environment. Others, like white tail deer, are able to live in a more general area.

The small deer live in more dense forests, and are rarely seen; bigger deer are more often seen.

The most deer are found in the Eurasian continent, meaning the combined area of Europe and Asia. There aren't as many varieties in America as there are in this area.

True deer versus other deer

There are some kinds of animals called deer that are not true deer.

A mouse deer.

There are two kinds of animals called deer that are not in the family Cervidae. These are the musk deer, and the mouse deer.

The musk deer is more primitive than a typical deer; it doesn't have the glands by its eyes, antlers, or as many teats. It also produces musk, which is valuable to humans.

A mouse deer is a very tiny animal that is nocturnal. It lives in Asia and Africa, and is never much bigger than a small dog, if that. They are not considered true deer. Instead, they are truly chevrotains, a kind of animal that is very small and sort of resembles a deer.

There are about ten species of chevrotains, and the mouse deer is the biggest. Males are very aggressive towards each other, though the female mouse deer are bigger.

Muntjac

Muntjacs are small deer that are also known as barking deer.

A Chinese muntjac.

This kind of deer is one of the oldest known types of deer; their remains were first found in France, Germany, and other parts of Europe. Now, however, they live in Asia, in places such as India, Japan, Indonesia, China, and other places.

Some muntjacs, however, live in England; they aren't native, but some escaped and some were released and they were introduced into the country. Now, they have spread from England to Wales.

A muntjac has shorter antlers than many bigger deer, without parts branching off. However, unlike most male deer, they don't use their antlers to fight; instead, they use their tusks, which are jutting out sort of teeth.

The Indian muntjac is polygamous; this means that more than one female is 'married' to a male. It also tends to have fur that is anywhere from brown to grayish to yellowish.

Chinese muntjacs are known to eat trees. Their faces are striped, and they are the sort of muntjac that is most commonly living in England and Wales. The Taiwanese version of this muntjac tend to have darker coats than the mainland Chinese ones.

The giant muntjac is the largest kind of muntjac. The problem for it is that it's endangered because in its habitat, the forest is burned in a technique known as slash and burn technique.

White-tailed deer

The white-tailed deer is a medium-size deer native to most of the Americas. It is very present in most of the United States, though more commonly East of the Rocky Mountains than West of them.

A white-tailed deer. This one is a buck.

White-tailed deer are probably what many American and Canadian children are familiar with as deer, despite the fact that moose and other deer are also present.

It's probably not a surprise, but the reason the white-tailed deer is called that is because it has a white tail. Not all deer have white tails.

The Western population of the white-tailed deer is a bit endangered, but towards the East, the population has only gotten bigger as coniferous (trees that don't lose their leaves every year, such as the pine trees) trees are cut down and more deciduous (trees that lose their leaves) trees and other plants grow in their place. This means more food for deer, and they've spread farther than ever before.

When a white-tailed deer is alarmed, it will raise its tail to alert other deer.

White-tailed deer are bigger in more temperate climates; if the climate is more tropical, such as in Florida, they will be smaller.

One interesting thing is that deer's vision is dichromatic, meaning 'two color'; they primarily see blue and yellow, but not red or orange, unlike humans. This is why hunters will usually use orange gear so that they aren't mistaken for prey, but are still able to hide from the deer.

Sometimes buck will end up without branching antlers, unlike most white-tailed bucks. These are called 'spikehorns' because they look like spikes. Also, very young male deer will have short knobs on their heads, the very beginning of them growing their own antlers. These aren't spikes.

Very, very rarely, a female will have antlers, but usually it's a little unclear whether it is truly a male or a female.

One interesting thing that white-tailed deer can eat is poison ivy! It doesn't bother them the same way it would bother a human, because a white-tailed deer's digestive system can handle things humans can't.

Roe deer

The roe deer lives in Europe throughout the whole continent, except too far north in Scandinavia and on several islands (Ireland, Iceland, and Mediterranean islands).

A pair of roe deer.

Roe deer are the subject of some of the Grimm brothers' collected fairy tales; roe deer have long been in Europe.

The roe deer that we're talking about is the Western roe deer; the Siberian roe deer is bigger and distinctly different. The Western roe deer is small, has very short antlers, and has reddish and gray fur.

A roe deer is crepuscular, meaning they are typically awake during twilight hours, such as dawn and dusk.

They have rump patches of white fur, heart-shaped on females and kidney-shaped on males. All their babies have white spots on their bodies.

A roe deer will usually only live to about 10 years old.

Like the muntjac, the roe deer is polygamous. Males will fight over females during mating season.

When a roe doe has babies, she typically has two, one boy and one girl. It is up to her to take care of her babies, because like with most deer species, the roe buck is no help at all.

Moose

The moose goes by either moose in North America or Eurasian Elk in Europe. It is the largest of the deer, and it lives in both Europe and North America in the colder North, but some varieties of moose live in Asia too.

A bull moose in Canada.

Moose are generally very slow-moving and sedentary (meaning staying in one place); however, if they are threatened, they can move pretty fast and be very dangerous.

Because moose are so big, the males are called bulls instead of bucks, and females are called cows instead of does. A baby is called a calf.

The interesting thing about a moose's antlers (which only the males have) is the way they are shaped. Instead of dendritic (which means branch-like), the moose has a palmate (meaning palm-shaped) antler; these are typically pretty big, and male moose can get very aggressive towards each other and use these antlers to fight.

Usually, the reason male moose fight is over a cow.

Moose are not like other deer in another way: they are very solitary creatures. They don't form herds. A mother will stay with her calf, but that's about it.

Moose only live in the North of Europe, Asia, and North America, but attempts have been made, in 1910 and the 1990s, to introduce them to New Zealand. However, both attempts failed.

Elk

Elk live in East Asia and in North America; they are known not only as elk, but by the Native American name 'wapiti'. They are some of the largest in the deer family.

A bull elk.

he elk has a rump patch, bigger than its cousin, the red deer of Europe. They have smaller tails than the mule deer, a sort of deer that lives in North America to the West.

Like moose, they are also called bulls, cows, and calves. This is very common for very large deer.

Elk are not as solitary as moose; they live in groups that are made up of either males or females; the genders don't mix unless it is mating season.

A form of screaming they do, that can be heard over miles, is called bugling. It is done by males to attract mates. It is a very distinctive sound, sort of similar to how a wolf howl is so easily identified.

Elk tend to live about 10 to 15 years in the wild, but in captivity, such as in a zoo, they might live to be twenty or more.

They also migrate every year, from higher ground to lower ground and back again, depending on the season. They follow the melting snow.

Fallow deer

Fallow deer come in a few different colors, and have been introduced all over the world, including in the United States of America.

http://www.123rf.com/photo_7859721_fallow-deer-in-the-wilderness-black-forest-germany.html?term=fallow%20deer

A fallow deer buck.

A fallow deer can come in one of four color varieties:

Common: this means a chestnut color with a mottle sort of white in the summer and a dark coat in the winter.

Menil: this means that they have spots all year round, though their coat does get darker in the winter.

Melanistic: this means they are black all year round, with no spots. They may be more of a gray-brown, depending on the individual deer.

Leucistic: this means they are white. They aren't albinos, and tend not to have the problems that come with albinism, because it's a natural color for them to be rather than a mutation of their genes.

Fallow deer stay in large groups, sometimes even over 100 of them in one group. Fallow deer are called bucks, does, and fawns, because they are a smaller sort of deer. Not a small deer in general, not compared to animals such as the muntjac, but they certainly aren't the largest deer around.

A fallow buck's antlers aren't dendritic; instead, they are palmate, shaped like shovels.

They are very fast and agile, though they can't run for as long as some other kinds of deer because they are not as muscular.

The fallow deer is native to Europe, but as before mentioned, it has been introduced all over the world. It is a very popular type of deer to put into new environments.

Brocket

A brocket is a South and North American deer. They have stout bodies and their ears are large compared to other deer.

http://www.123rf.com/photo_7112911_group-of-young-brockets-lying-on-the-grass.html?term=brocket

A group of young brockets.

There are ten species of brocket, and most live in South America, some on Trinidad island, others in places like Peru and Colombia. Brockets are a medium or small sized deer. However, some also live in Central America and North America.

They are nocturnal and very shy; this means they are rarely seen. Not as much is known about them as deer such as white-tailed deer or moose. Instead of running away from predators, they tend to hide in the plants of the area, since they know their territory so well.

Often, two brockets, a male and a female, will become a monogamous pair (meaning that they only have fawns together, not with other brockets). However, a single male brocket may end up mating with many female deer and not becoming a pair with any of them.

The fawns are kept out of side by the mother until they are old enough to come with them. Brocket fawns are weaned (not drinking their mother's milk anymore, and instead eating 'adult' food) at around six months. In only a year, they are adults.

Pudu

Pudu are the smallest kind of deer.

http://www.123rf.com/photo_8534988_southern-pudu-pudu-puda.html?term=pudu

A southern pudu.

The pudu has two subspecies, Northern and Southern. They both live in South America, though, as you might guess, one lives in more the Northern part of South America and the other in the more Southern part.

The Northern is the smaller one, by about 10 centimeters. It also weighs less, and its antlers don't get as big as the Southern's. The Northern also lives in higher areas than the Southern.

Pudus are very secretive creatures who live alone; it's because of this that they are hard to find, and little is known about how they act. However, it is known what they look like, often with reddish-brown fur and spike antlers on the males, as well as slender legs. They tend to be somewhere in between 30-45 centimeters in height.

They tend to zigzag when running away, because they are very agile creatures. It often throws off followers, because they are able to climb very well.

Right now, pudus, both species, are endangered because of habitats being destroyed and being overhunted.

Conclusion

Deer are amazing creatures. They have long captured the imagination of people throughout the world, and been used as symbols even by modern day people (such as in the flag of Michigan).

From Bambi to the hunter in Artemis's myth, the deer will continue to be present in the human mind for a long time to come.

Author Bio

Rachel Smith is a young author who enjoys animals. Once, she had a rabbit who was very nervous, and chewed through her leash and tried to escape. She's also had several pet mice, who were the funniest little animals to watch. She lives in Ohio with her family and writes in her spare time.

Our books are available at

1. Amazon.com

2. Barnes and Noble

3. Itunes

4. Kobo

5. Smashwords

6. Google Play Books

This book is published by

JD-Biz Corp

P O Box 374

Mendon, Utah 84325

http://www.jd-biz.com/

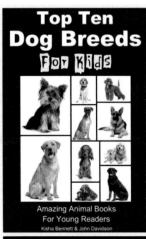

Top Ten Dog Breeds For Kids

Amazing Animal Books
For Young Readers
Kisha Bennett & John Davidson

Poodles

Dog Books for Kids
K. Bennett

Labrador Retrievers

Dog Books for Kids
K. Bennett

German Shepherds

Dog Books for Kids
K. Bennett

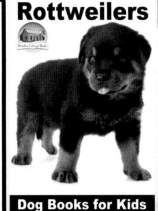

Rottweilers

Dog Books for Kids
K. Bennett

Boxers

Dog Books for Kids
K. Bennett

Golden Retrievers

Dog Books for Kids
K. Bennett

Beagles

Dog Books for Kids
K. Bennett

Yorkies

Dog Books for Kids
K. Bennett

Made in the USA
Monee, IL
18 October 2021